CHARLESTON COME HELL
OR
HIGH WATER

A HISTORY IN PHOTOGRAPHS

Photographs collected by
ROBERT N. S. WHITELAW

Text by
ALICE F. LEVKOFF

Published by
Alice F. Levkoff and Patti F. Whitelaw
Charleston, South Carolina

A self-portrait by Robert N.S. Whitelaw made at the age of twenty-two while serving as photographer for Dr. William Beebe, Director of Tropical Research, on the Bermuda Oceanographical Expedition of the New York Zoological Society.

COVER PHOTOGRAPH — National Archives, Brady Collection.

The Exchange Building, a portrayal done by a Brady photographer shortly after the Confederates evacuated the city during the Civil War, best represents the resiliency of Charleston. Built in 1767-1771 while Carolina was still a British colony, the Exchange has served the community for over two centuries.

Mathew Brady, one of America's first photographers of renown, was noted for sending teams of photographers along with Union troops during the Civil War.

Introduction

From his childhood, Robert N.S. Whitelaw was good at making things with his hands. I first knew him when we were teen-agers growing up in Charleston. Model airplanes were the fashion among boys around the time of World War I. Bob was a craftsman in neatly assembling models from the kits we bought or received as birthday presents. He could handle the delicate bits of wood and paper without getting himself hopelessly stuck together with glue. Even then he was acquiring skills and developing powers of observation that were to make him one of the country's best known constructors of dioramas.

Bob Whitelaw's work is represented in half a dozen museums and other public exhibitions. In the model airplane days, at age thirteen, he hung around the Charleston Museum, picking up information about a variety of things.

His interests were wide, and he had a flair for display. During the twenty-three years he was director of the Carolina Art Association he devised novel ways of showing paintings and promoting the arts. Among the memorable exhibitions he assembled at the Gibbes Art Gallery were Fraser miniatures (1934), the Kress Collection of Renaissance Art (1935) and the Solomon R. Guggenheim Collection (1936), shown in public for the first time at the Gibbes.

When the Association was given custody of the Dock Street Theatre, he became the producer of plays that brought new dimensions to the community stage of Charleston.

During his time as director, the Carolina Art Association published *This is Charleston*, the first inventory of important local architecture. Though he had many helpers, it was his book, and it turned out to be a useful tool for preservation during the early days of a nationally acclaimed movement to save old houses. He also promoted an off-street parking plan, procured by the art association, which might have rejuvenated the King Street shopping center in downtown Charleston had it been adopted during the 1930's.

Bob Whitelaw was endowed with an active mind, a keen artistic sense and the urge to make use of them. He left a rich legacy through his work for Charleston that was not fully recognized in his lifetime. This book of photographs, which he did not live to finish, was the last of his projects. It is another expression of a lifelong love affair with Charleston, the city of his birth.

Thomas R. Waring

Acknowledgments

The concept of *Charleston—Come Hell or High Water* and its collection of photographs were the work of Robert N.S. Whitelaw. The text of the book was contributed by Alice F. Levkoff. All information has been checked for accuracy to the best available knowledge.

A hearty thanks is extended to the superb staffs and resources of the Charleston Library Society, the South Carolina Historical Society, the Charleston County Library, the Gibbes Art Gallery, and many unnamed kind individuals. The helpful editorial comments of Dr. Joseph Waring and Maizie-Louise Rubin are gratefully acknowledged. Special recognition is accorded the late Helen McCormack for her valuable guidance and William Jordan of the *News and Courier* staff for the preparation of photographic material.

Copyright © 1976

Alice F. Levkoff, Charleston, S.C.

Library of Congress Catalog Number 75-27713

ISBN 0-9619665-0-5

PRINTED AND BOUND IN THE U.S.A.

Preface

The charisma of Charleston defies definition. Its past three centuries are interwoven with a variety of moods which span the entire spectrum of human sensitivity. The first English settlers found a land pleasant for living but not without its liabilities. In addition to hostile Indians and threatening Spaniards they fought disease and devastating storms. Even the mundane annoyances of recurrent flooding at high tide, constant infiltration by clouds of clamoring insects, and uncomfortably torrid summers did not curtail Charleston's growth. Its populace survived economic highs and lows with patience and fortitude. Bombardment and military occupation followed by poverty and political chaos served only to stiffen the backbone of these enthusiastic citizens. Can we conclude that Charleston really displays its strength best in the face of disaster?

Whatever the answer we must also state that the Charlestonian has perfected the art of graciously enjoying all of life's pleasures. As one lady "from away" observed at the beginning of the twentieth century:

> It is said that what makes for the real happiness of a Charlestonian is his utter contentment. He is convinced that South Carolina is the best state in the Union, that Charleston is, of course, the greatest city in South Carolina, and that his own family is the best family in Charleston. Sometimes he even goes a step further and considers himself the most important member of his family. It is a most enviable state of mind but it causes the outsider, perhaps, to feel a little aggrieved at times. The feeling of contentment or superiority is so self-satisfying to the possessor, however, that nobody but a brute would wish to rob him of it.

> Another reason for his contentment, perhaps, is the ease of life in Charleston. The climate is delightful, the place abounds in picturesque surroundings of historic interest, the waters are full of the finest fish, the forests are filled with the best of game, with the earliest vegetables and fruits and with splendid old Southern cookery.

> —Daisy Breaux, *Autobiography of A Chameleon*

And so we might then ask, what is a Charlestonian anyway? One who is Charleston-born with, at least, a set of grandparents sleeping peacefully in a nearby graveyard. Or perhaps, one whose parents had the good sense to move here in time for his birth. But could not a late-comer with love in his heart just slip in under the wire?

Herein, for *all* "Charlestonophiles", lies photographic testimony of the city's stubborn resistance to a century of catastrophe which has culminated finally into the present burst of glory!

Alice F. Levkoff
Charleston, South Carolina
June 1, 1974

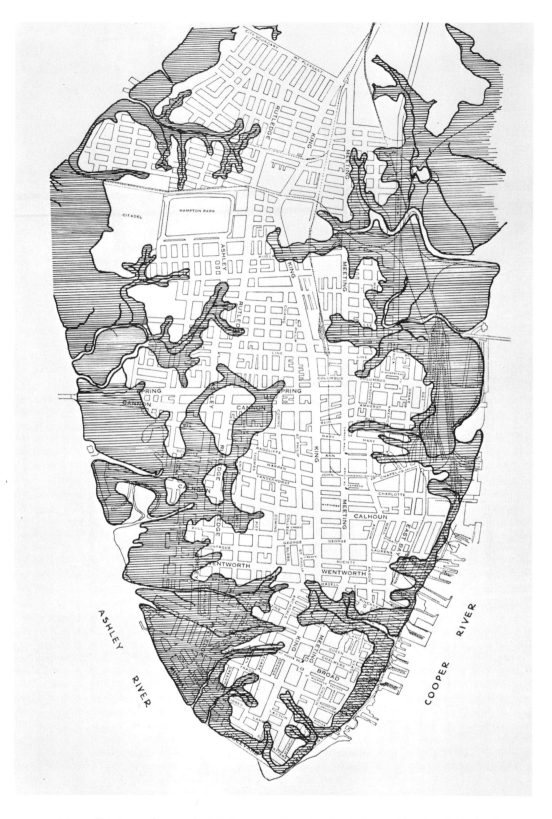

* from *This Is Charleston*, published by the Carolina Art Association (Gibbes Art Gallery), Charleston, South Carolina, 1944.

Charleston's distinctive reputation for changelessness belies the original boundaries of its high land. Even a hasty glance at the map on the opposite page verifies the enormous amount of fill on which it now sits. The unshaded area depicts the natural contours of the convoluted shoreline that first met the gaze of the English settlers over 300 years ago.

The growing population's need for more living space happily meshed with the disposal problem created by the mountains of debris deposited by Charleston's periodic fires and fierce storms. All the wreckage was dumped into the most convenient marsh or creek, and slowly one finger of high ground was joined to another, creating a new neighborhood.

As early as 1717, land fill operations had already begun when the moat which surrounded portions of the old walled city was filled. Water Street was truly liquid until after the Revolutionary War. The City Market stands on low and boggy ground which was filled in the early part of the nineteenth century. As Charleston's economy became more sophisticated, the residues of its thriving industries became the basis of "made land." Many a house sits on a foundation of sawdust and woodchips, and one even rests on the site of an old palmetto log fortification.

The shorelines of both the Ashley and the Cooper Rivers have gradually expanded, and the filling-in process still continues today when developers, environmentalists, and a host of governmental bodies agree. However, the net result is often inaction, so perhaps Charleston is finally complete—except, of course, for silt deposits, hurricanes, earthquakes, tornadoes, erosion, and other acts of God!

Charleston Museum

The age of photography was ushered in when Louis Jacques Mandé Daguerre sold his process for permanently fixing images onto a polished plate to the French government in 1839. The new invention quickly crossed the Atlantic and Americans took to the daguerreotype immediately. By the mid-1840's technical improvements brought the camera to every country hamlet, and hundreds of galleries opened with Charleston having its share. The shiny copper plate exposed to the light of the sun produced inexpensive portraiture, taken up enthusiastically by the public.

However, the daguerreotype was replaced in the early 1860's with a new photographic process, the wet plate. This procedure, using a glass plate dipped in a chemical solution which had to be exposed and developed immediately, proved to be more complex. But one advantage over its predecessor outweighed the trouble—that of being able to make more than one print from each exposure. Thus, the golden age of daguerreotype photography lost its luster when the era of the negative and its vast quantity of paper prints arrived, the same process that is still in use today.

The camera catches a covey of Charlestonians—all forever nameless . . . a youthful equestrian, an aspiring artist, and a voracious reader with one book in his hand and another under his elbow!

Charleston Museum

Susan Pringle Alston, pictured above, is dressed in the height of the late 50's fashion. She traveled abroad with her father and brother in 1859; perhaps this is a Paris gown. At least we know she had her portrait done; the pastel still hangs in the family home at 21 East Battery (The Edmondston-Alston House) with its French label intact.

Even the threat of approaching hostilities didn't seem to curb the popularity of portrait photography. Just before the bombardment of Fort Sumter the governor of South Carolina appeared at breakfast in Charleston dressed ready for a ball with swallow-tail and all. He announced to his astonished friends that he was not going mad but to the photographer's, and this is the way his wife wanted him attired!

An ante-bellum (1853) view of a tree-lined avenue in the gardens of Magnolia-on-the-Ashley. Paradoxically, ill health was the spur that led to the creation of the profuse beauty associated with the gardens. The onslaught of tuberculosis removed the Reverend John Drayton from his chosen field, and he turned to outdoor work as an aid to recovery, thus developing a simple plantation garden into a natural wonderland. Imported azaleas and camellias found their happy home in the Low Country climate where they have been thriving ever since. At one time a plaque in London's Kew Gardens attributed azaleas "in their highest glory to Magnolia Gardens, near Charleston, South Carolina, U. S. A."

An interesting sidelight to Mr. Drayton's Magnolia inheritance is that, by stipulation of the will, he had to change his name to carry on that of his maternal grandfather; John Grimke became John Grimke-Drayton. Under a South Carolina law which had been passed to ease such transfers, this, apparently, was not an uncommon practice.

Meeting Street looking north from Chalmers Street before 1861.

Robert Mills's magnificent Circular Congregational Church dominates the background. The Roman Corinthian portico led into a rotunda ninety feet in diameter, and Mr. Mills claimed that its dome was the first built in America. (See page 133.)

The glorious Renaissance palace next door, the South Carolina Institute Hall was constructed in 1853. Here, on that fateful December evening in 1860, the ordinance of secession was signed.

Alas, our loss—this entire block lay in the path of the destructive fire of 1861.

The year is 1846, and "Honest Abe" has just been elected to his first national office, a seat in the House of Representatives. This earliest likeness of Abraham Lincoln from a daguerreotype is attributed to N. B. Shepherd of Springfield, Illinois.

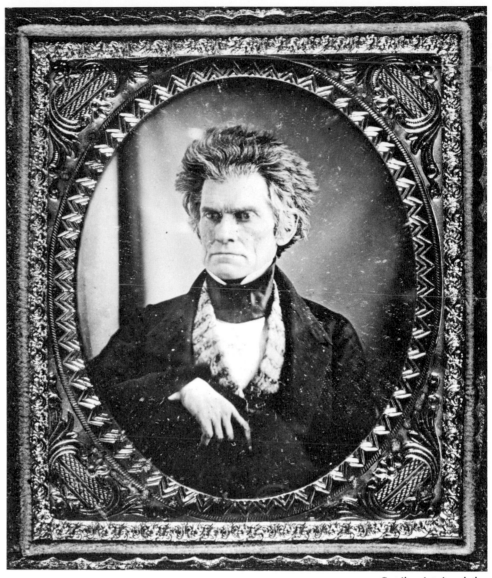

John C. Calhoun's concern about the dilemma the South faced—that it could have either slavery or the Union but there was little hope of both—is reflected in his worry-lined face. This daguerreotype, taken in his later years, had been given to a friend in Congress.

Active on the national scene from the War of 1812 until his death, this South Carolinian's political philosophy echoed the feeling of the region as it slowly shifted from nationalism to sectionalism.

The gulf which divided the views of the two men pictured on these pages became so untenable that the country's worst conflagration resulted, the Civil War. However, before the final break came, Calhoun died, and, in April of 1850, all Charleston paid homage to him when the city literally draped itself in mourning for his funeral and burial in St. Philip's churchyard.

The seeds of secession sown by John Calhoun in 1832 with the nullification issue were fed through the succeeding years by knotty economic problems in the South and the growing abolition movement in the North. The election of Abraham Lincoln to the presidency only served to increase the South's apprehensions. On December 20, 1860, the Hall of Saint Andrew's Society provided the assembly room for the state convention which passed the ordinance of secession, marking the end of South Carolina's union with the United States.

When Confederate forces fired on the federal supply boat *Star of the West* and followed this with the bombardment of Fort Sumter in April 1861, they initiated a series of events which culminated in four years of tragic warfare between the states. Charleston, where it all began, fought valiantly only to endure defeat and years of difficult recovery afterward.

The ruins of the Hall of Saint Andrew's Society are pictured on the opposite page. Charleston's oldest benevolent society was founded in 1729 to assist all people in distress, and its hall stood directly in the path of the great fire of December 1861. A small cooking blaze which got out of control on Hasell Street spread westward over the peninsula, decimating almost a third of the city. Union cannon fire contributed more damage during the war years to the lower portion of Charleston.

Erected in 1815, only the bare walls of the Hall of the Saint Andrew's Society at 118 Broad Street remained in 1865.

9

Mathew Brady's war photographers came to Charleston along with the Union forces after the city had been evacuated by the Confederates in February 1865, and this is one scene that greeted them. A northern newspaper correspondent painted his view in words:

> A city of ruins, of desolation, of vacant houses, of widowed women, of rotting wharves, of deserted warehouses, of weed-wild gardens, of miles of grass-grown streets, of acres of pitiful and voiceful barrenness—that is Charleston, wherein Rebellion loftily reared its head five years ago.
> —Sidney Andrews, *The South Since the War*

Looking south on Meeting Street toward Saint Michael's Church and the ruins of the Circular Congregational Church, both sides of the street have been almost leveled from the fire of 1861 and the bombardment.

The noble Pinckney mansion stands here in skeletal condition close to the area where the fire started. Dating from c. 1747, the house was located on Colleton Square just north of the City Market where it commanded a fine view of the Cooper River. Charles Pinckney drew the plans himself, and over 300,000 Carolina-made brick were used in its construction. Both he and his second wife, Eliza Lucas, made lasting contributions to the Carolina colony, and their progeny has continued in the family tradition of government and community service.

This 1865 view of lower Meeting Street looks north from South Battery. Note the earthworks in the middle of the thoroughfare, probably part of the unfinished inner ring of city defenses.

Right—The earthwork defenses in White Point Garden are pictured in 1865. The upper picture shows the King Street Battery taken from behind the wrought iron fence of a South Battery residence. The cannons in the lower photo are pointed out to the harbor from their location at the foot of East Battery.

Fort Sumter, a view from the sand bar, shows the exterior about 1865. Named for one of South Carolina's most illustrious soldiers of the Revolution, General Thomas Sumter, the fort was part of a chain of coastal fortifications built by the federal government. Begun in 1829, it was not completely finished when Major Robert Anderson moved in after the passage of the ordinance of secession in December 1860. The fort was surrendered to Confederate forces the following April and was held by them throughout hostilities until February 1865.

This interior view of Fort Sumter in 1861 was probably taken by George S. Cook of Charleston. The "Stars and Bars", one of the flags flown by the Confederacy, flies above the fort. This flag had the disarming disadvantage of being confused with the Union flag from a distance on the battlefield.

A view of Castle Pinckney from the seaside in 1865 shows its location on a harbor island, Shute's Folly, just off shore from Charleston. This isle had been the location of a battery since 1780. Earlier records indicate that a tea house occupied the site until it was washed away in the gale of 1752. Named in honor of Charles Cotesworth Pinckney, at the end of the eighteenth century when he returned home after serving as Ambassador to France, the present fort was constructed for the War of 1812. It was in the process of being fortified by the United States Corps of Engineers when three companies of South Carolina troops seized it in December 1860, on the eve of the Civil War.

Federal prisoners captured at Bull Run and interned at Castle Pinckney were photographed in August 1861 by George S. Cook. Castle Pinckney played a small role in the Civil War, being used only for a prison and later for storage.

A Brady picture shows the interior of Fort Moultrie on Sullivan's Island looking north toward Battery Beauregard. The fort was named after Colonel William Moultrie who successfully defended the original palmetto-log outpost against the British in an early decisive battle of the Revolutionary War. The use of those famous "cannon-ball repelling" tree trunks is still in evidence as pictured in the wall, right foreground.

Fort Moultrie, the view looking west across Sullivan's Sound, was evacuated by federal forces in December 1860, when Major Robert Anderson moved his entire garrison to Fort Sumter. It is interesting to note that the major's father served here in 1779, during the Revolutionary War.

After Major Anderson's departure South Carolina troops seized the fort, important in the bombardment of Fort Sumter four months later, and it played an active part in the defense of Charleston. Batteries Beauregard, Bee, and Marshall were built by Confederate forces on the island farther northeast.

An 1865 view of Fort Johnson on James Island shows the ring of cannons pointing toward the mouth of the harbor. A fort was located on this point of land as early as 1704, and many successive ones followed. Since federal forces did not consider this installation valuable, South Carolina troops easily moved in shortly after taking Fort Moultrie. Although its strength was built up to twenty-six guns and some mortars, the fort was involved in only one major skirmish, repulsing a Union force from Morris Island in 1864. Along with the other harbor forts, Confederate forces evacuated it in February 1865.

Looking across Charleston Harbor toward Castle Pinckney, this interior view of Fort Johnson shows a line of chimneys in assorted stages of deterioration. They once warmed the quarters of troops stationed there. The cannons pictured on the opposite page stand on the far side of the earthworks.

The Confederacy's miracle weapon, designed to destroy the Union blockade of Charleston Harbor, sits on the pluff mud and oyster shells at the foot of Tradd Street on the Ashley River. This rusting relic, called "Little David", was one of about six semi-submersible gunboats that were built to carry a torpedo mounted on a bow spar. Their one success, a first in naval history, caused enough damage to the federal gunboat *New Ironsides* to send her back to Philadelphia for repairs. Rear Admiral John A. Dahlgren was extremely impressed with the potential threat of such a vessel.

The majestic John Ashe Alston house stands in the background dominating the northwest corner of Rutledge and Tradd Streets. Its Corinthian-columned entrance no longer faces the water but became landlocked after the turn of the century when the boulevard landfill project was completed. (See page 129.)

Empty, mysterious—East Battery seems drained of all its
vitality in this 1865 view.

William Tecumseh Sherman, General of the Union forces, was no stranger to the South. He had spent a few years at Fort Moultrie (1842-43, 1844-5) and enjoyed the friendship of local families. However, he could not accept the South's decision and pointed to South Carolina as the "hellhole of secession." His terrible march to the sea, leaving a nightmare of destruction in its wake, turned its route away from Charleston, and the city was spared that final desecration.

Rear Admiral John A. Dahlgren, the gentleman in the middle with his thumb hooked over his belt and a scowl on his face, stands on the deck of his flagship, the *USS New Ironsides*, outside Charleston Harbor. Credited with revolutionizing naval ordnance, he, more than any other person, was responsible for its proficiency during the Civil War.

Admiral Dahlgren was charged with maintaining a blockade in the waters of the southeast Atlantic, and his direction of federal ships successfully strangled Charleston's activities. The longest bombardment, 587 days, in the history of war took place and finally led to the Confederate evacuation of the harbor forts and the city.

24

Five Union generals, who were imprisoned in the O'Connor residence pictured left at 180 Broad Street, must have found these quarters quite comfortable. Given a fair amount of freedom of movement, they entertained themselves by playing ball at the end of the block around the banks of Colonial Lake, then called "The Pond." The Confederate strategy in housing them so close to the area of bombardment was to discourage Union forces from shelling the lower portion of the city, but unfortunately it was no deterrent.

The 1865 photograph below shows the clubhouse at Washington Race Track where federal officers were confined in Charleston during the Civil War. The building was the home of the South Carolina Jockey Club, the oldest jockey club in the United States. Charles F. Reichardt, prominent Charleston architect, designed this building, the grandstand, and other structures for the race course in 1837. The gate posts would later be given to Mr. August Belmont of New York to be used at the entrance of Belmont Park. Slated to open in 1906, this facility was to be the center of gentlemen's turf racing as Washington Park had been in earlier years.

Library of Congress, Brady Collection

East Battery in 1865 shows damage from the bombardment to the stately homes that line this harbor boulevard. Eternal hope springs anew in the row of small trees growing along the edge of the walkway. Caroline Gilman, the widow of the Charleston Unitarian minister, wrote in her diary after returning to Charleston in the spring of 1865:

"I could not help thinking yesterday, as I saw the flowers look up and smile . . . that they set us a good example politically. But then, flowers have no memory."

—George C. Rogers, Jr., *Charleston in the Age of the Pinckneys*

The exploded Blakeley gun, pictured right, is a close-up view of the same one seen in the foreground of the photograph above. It was one of two that crossed the Atlantic on Captain E. C. Reid's steamship *Sumter*. The length of the guns necessitated their being loaded in an upright position so that the steamer at sea gave the appearance of having three smoke stacks. Captain Reid ran the blockade successfully at Wilmington, North Carolina, in broad daylight and after a long, eventful trip, the cannon was finally mounted at White Point Garden. But unfortunately, it was never close enough to the enemy to be fired. In February 1865, when the city was evacuated, the cannon was burst to prevent its falling into the hands of the federal army. And a sizeable fragment of the gun lodged in the rafters of the roof of the Roper House at 9 East Battery where it still remains.

Vendue Range, looking west, appears lifeless, quite opposite from the bustling business atmosphere usually associated with this short block. Serving both as a site for local auctions and a passageway to the public docks, the imposing sidewalk colonnade provided Charleston merchants and pedestrians with protection against the heat of the sun and the discomfort of inclement weather.

In 1861, General Robert E. Lee stood on the second floor balcony of the Mills House watching the terrible fire that destroyed over 540 acres of the city. General P. G. T. Beauregard was also a guest of the hotel until the accuracy of federal shelling prompted his departure.

The hotel had been described by a local newspaper as "one of the largest and most commodious buildings in the city." Financed by Otis Mills of grain and real estate wealth, the five story structure with 125 rooms opened its doors in 1853. This photograph dates from 1865.

The South Carolina Society Hall stands on Meeting Street just above Tradd, and its handsome portico can be seen in the right foreground of this 1865 view.

The structure, dating from 1804, was erected by the South Carolina Society, a benevolent group who first began their good works in the early eighteenth century by agreeing to spend "two bits" regularly at a tavern operated by one of their French countrymen whose business needed bolstering.

Note Saint Michael's in the background, painted black to present a less obvious target for Union shells. This photograph was for use in the family stereopticon.

The ruins of Saint Finbar's and Saint John's Cathedral stand out in bold relief against the sky in this 1865 photograph. Located on the corner of Broad and Legare Streets a few blocks west of City Hall, this church was one of five destroyed in the fire of 1861, and ironically, its fire insurance is said to have lapsed just one week before!

Peace has returned . . . life goes on in Charleston. By 1880, the railings along the city's favorite promenade have been painted, and the Cooper River skyline is cross-hatched with schooner masts. A developing lumber boom is bringing prosperity to the port of Charleston where ships are waiting at the wharves to be loaded with export cargoes of wood.

The Bath House, c. 1880, from a double picture for the stereopticon, on the Ashley River is approached from White Point Garden by a long ramp. Although the location was very vulnerable to Charleston's frequent and destructive storms, a series of bath houses was built in this area. A notice in the May 3, 1845 issue of the *Charleston Mercury* described such a facility:

> This above Establishment will be open for the season THIS DAY, 1st instant. In addition to the former arrangements, the Ladies are respectfully informed that a building . . ., containing three more private Baths and one large Swimming Bath, has been erected especially for their accommodation.
> The Saloon and the upper part of the house will be furnished with ICED CREAMS, ICED FRUITS, SHERBERTS, PASTRY, etc. prepared in the very best manner, by Mr. Joseph Cropper, from Broadway, New York.

Salt water bathing was limited to such facilities unless one had the good fortune to travel to the island beaches. Bath houses were later constructed in other parts of Charleston, and they were operated by the city under strict rules and regulations, providing a means of healthful and refreshing recreation.

The sad, defeated mammal of the sea, a baleen whale, is pictured on Pregnall's Wharf on the Ashley River, January 8, 1880. Three days earlier the whale innocently swam into Charleston Harbor, and a battle of color and excitement followed which involved numerous local tugs and harpoonists. The spectacle was closely observed by hundreds of spectators who lined up on High Battery to observe these remarkable proceedings.

Post-Courier, Charleston, South Carolina

The whale's carcass, forty feet four inches in length, was towed away to the beach. After its skeleton was exposed, it was wired together and suspended from the ceiling of the Charleston Museum where generations of local children long remember it. The photograph above was taken when the Museum's collections were housed on the third floor of the main building of the College of Charleston. Colonel Edward B. White, the versatile local architect, had enlarged the building for the museum's purpose some years earlier. (See page 53.)

National Archives, United States Coast Guard

The photograph of the Charleston Main Light on Morris Island was taken on June 6, 1885, by Major Jared C. Smith. Rebuilt in 1876, the magnitude of the tower's construction follows: it stands 158 feet above sea level, measuring 33 feet in diameter at the base and 16 feet, 8 inches at the neck of the cornice. An iron staircase of nine flights ascends the tower which rests on a foundation of 264 piles. The light is visible for 18¾ nautical miles.

Originally established in 1767, this light had graduated from open braziers filled with "fier balls of pitch and ocum" to tallow candles, and then on to sperm oil burned in a sort of Argand lamp (named after its Swiss inventor). The lighting apparatus at the time of this photograph consisted of a reflector system including a double lens apparatus with lights burning both lard and mineral oil.

National Archives, United States Coast Guard

On the same day, Major Smith also took this picture of the assistant keeper's dwelling with two uniformed attendants in view. This site had provided beacons to guide ships in and out of Charleston Harbor for many decades. As early as 1789 the newly formed United States of America accepted jurisdiction over the already existing lighthouses on the coast, eight in number. The Charleston Main Light was the only one in the South.

A full scale model of "The Best Friend" is photographed about 1927. Appropriately named with the high hope of becoming Charleston's best friend by bringing a great volume of cotton export traffic to the home port, the train made its first successful run in December 1830. A year earlier, with the encouragement of both the City Council and the Chamber of Commerce, the South Carolina Canal and Railroad Company had constructed an experimental railroad on the corner of Smith and Wentworth Streets. Six miles of road were subsequently built on which a number of initial runs, carrying five to six cars of forty to fifty passengers at sixteen to twenty-one miles per hour, were completed. But, unfortunately, just six months later, the Best Friend's promising career came to an abrupt end with the explosion of its boiler.

Drayton Hall, from the land side, is portrayed with its flankers still extant in a photograph taken by Cook some years before the earthquake. Built between 1738 and 1742, this palatial Palladian villa has survived in almost pristine condition, and remains the only complete plantation house on the west bank of the Ashley River. General Sherman's stragglers, who laid waste to the neighborhood, stayed away from Drayton Hall when they learned it was being used as a pest house for smallpox victims.

The residence is said to have cost $90,000 with much of the fine material imported from England. The letters of Eliza Lucas Pinckney, dating from colonial years in Carolina, refer to "a festal day" spent with Mrs. Drayton of Drayton Hall.

Historic Charleston Foundation

The great cyclone of 1885 hit on the morning of August 25, with a fury not remembered! East Battery is pictured above.

Great Waves, rolling inward without resistance struck the sea wall of the Battery in swift succession, with a deafening roar, and, bursting into huge water-spouts were hurled against the fronts of residences along the street smashing in windows and doors, leveling fences and inundating the lawns and gardens.

Evidence for this calamitous quotation from the *Charleston Yearbook of 1885* had been provided by Cook's Photograph Gallery at 265 King Street. George LaGrange Cook undoubtedly took the photographs on these pages. His father had already moved from the city, and George would join him shortly, ending almost forty years of Cook photography in Charleston.

Right—Flood tides of inconceivable force swept private yachts onto South Battery (top) where the water reached the depth of six feet and destroyed the adjacent boat slips at the foot of King Street (below).

Charlestonians were just beginning to breathe a sigh of relief after the recovery from the cyclone of the previous year when, on the evening of August 31, 1886, about fifteen minutes before ten o'clock, the greatest earthquake ever recorded in eastern United States struck! Successive tremors followed for thirty-six hours, generating agony amongst Charleston's fifty thousand inhabitants which left them shivering with shock. Local citizens immediately sought open places for safety from falling walls and other flying debris. Makeshift shelters were set up in the city's parks which provided housing until the tremors stopped and building repairs could be initiated.

The fault producing the earthquake, Woodstock by name, ran from Summerville to a great distance at sea. Huge fissures appeared out of which boiled great geysers of mud and water reaching heights of twenty to thirty feet. Railroad tracks on end and strange rifts cutting into the roads made traveling in and out of Charleston impossible for several days. But when news of the disaster reached the world, help generously poured in from all the states and many distant quarters of the globe. The only exception, a questioning letter received from Chicago's Mayor Harrison, included portions of an official report written by a Colonel Batchelder which stated: ". . . the earthquake is a benefit to them (the working classes) for it provides them with plenty of employment at far higher wages than they were earning before."

However, the need for aid could not be better demonstrated than by the final tally of property damage which amounted to six million dollars. Immediate deaths numbered from twenty-seven to thirty, with over sixty fatalities resulting from injuries, altogether a remarkably small number considering the crowded urban area affected.

Not without its commercial value, the earthquake prompted the publication of a number of albums filled with photographs of the destruction. The preface of one states, "Not as an advertising scheme but an artistic souvenir fit for any parlor or library." Many of the photographs, including the ones to follow, were taken by George L. Cook, and one hopes he employed the dry plate technique, a new photographic method surpassing the wet plate in ease and efficiency.

Another popular souvenir was a collection of seven bottles, each containing a different color of sand spewed out from the fissures. A set, selling for one dollar, embellished every Low Country mantel for years to come.

Charlestonians, with their usual courage and fortitude, dug out from the ruins and began to rebuild the city again.

The portico of Hiberian Hall at 105 Meeting Street was so badly wrecked that nothing remained of it. Broken columns and fragments of their capitals add to the piles of debris surrounding the front of the building.

43

Roper Hospital, below, and the Medical College of the State of South Carolina, opposite, occupied the east and west corners of the same block on Queen Street. This area suffered the worst damage of the earthquake, and the building was never used as a hospital again. One hundred patients, one of whom was killed, were interned here on the Mazyck Street corner (now Logan Street) at the time of the shock. The hospital's center portion eventually lived on as the Marlboro Apartments.

The Medical College of South Carolina opened in 1824 and two years later occupied this building designed by Frederick Wesner, a Charleston architect. Attached to this was an infirmary which probably represented the first such structure erected particularly for clinical teaching purposes. The building was repaired after the quake and served the faculty and students until 1913 when they moved into a new facility at Barre and Calhoun Streets.

Local physicians' efforts to keep Charleston's populace in tip-top health were aided, and perhaps abetted, with two remarkable products manufactured on Market Street by Keppel Kurnitzki. According to an 1886 advertisement, Wire Grass Tonic took care of dyspepsia and asthma while its companion, Wire Grass Liver Medicine, cured catarrh and all complaints of the blood, liver, lungs and stomach!

The Old Guard House and Police Station on the southwest corner of Meeting and Broad Streets was eventually torn down as a result of damage from the quake. Thirty men sleeping in the upper story at the time escaped unhurt. The building served as headquarters for the city police and as confinement quarters for arrested prisoners awaiting trial. About a decade later the United States Post Office was constructed on this same site.

In the next block eastward, one finds W. W. Smith, stencil works, and its neighbor, Cigars & Tobacco, with their upper facades denuded!

The Holmes house appears to have suffered only a few minor cracks; its appealing exterior remained intact as shown in this post-earthquake photograph. The earliest dwelling constructed in this block, c. 1820, it stands just south of the Edmondston-Alston house and the two must have made an exceedingly handsome pair on East Battery.

Unfortunately, the house did not weather the wind and water destruction of the hurricane of 1911 as well as the tremors of the '86 quake. Irreparable damage occurred which, combined with the neglect of being unoccupied, resulted in its having been torn down c. 1913 . . . what a pity!

The Orphan House Chapel on Vanderhorst Street exhibits some exterior cracks but little of its fine facade has been disturbed. Built in 1802, the chapel was designed by Charleston's celebrated amateur architect, Gabriel Manigault, who also drew the designs for his brother Joseph's dwelling, the City Hall and the South Carolina Society Hall.

In the middle of the 1950's this gem of "national architectural importance" (below) was torn down to make way for another parking lot.

Two buildings with wooden props shoring up their walls are awaiting repair. The Exchange Building, above, had already lost its cupola and balustrade in 1883, and the quake dislodged its decorative roof urns.

China Hall located on the street level of the Odd Fellows Hall on King Street appears to be open for business as usual.

The steeple of Saint Philip's Church on Church Street was saved by the courage and skill of three Charleston mechanics. They ascended the tower and removed the fallen debris and broken ornamental pillars, exposing the true supporting timbers shown above. Damage to the roof had been inflicted at the time of the quake by falling iron columns and bricks from the steeple. The total repair cost came to $20,000.

Bennett's Rice Mill located on the shore of the Cooper River suffered extensive damage from the earthquake. Scaffolding indicates that repairs are underway. The structure dates from 1844, and its Palladian styling exemplifies the Low Country's fine industrial architecture.

Most of the damage to the College of Charleston's main building appears to be confined to the wings. The center portion was built from a design by William Strickland of Philadelphia in 1828, forty-three years after the college was chartered. The wings and portico were added about two decades later from plans by Charleston architect, Edward B. White.

Charleston Library Society

A "tent city" located in Washington Park next to City Hall is pictured above. Families lived in this fashion while their homes were being repaired after the earthquake. After life returned to normal, the city fathers reportedly grumbled that the parks were left a shambles, no doubt as if an earthquake had struck them!

The tent floor of a more affluent Charleston family is covered with an oriental carpet. "Dah",* the family retainer, remains at the helm of the household with her charges at her side.

---

* Dah was a local generic name customarily ascribed to the most important family nursemaid.

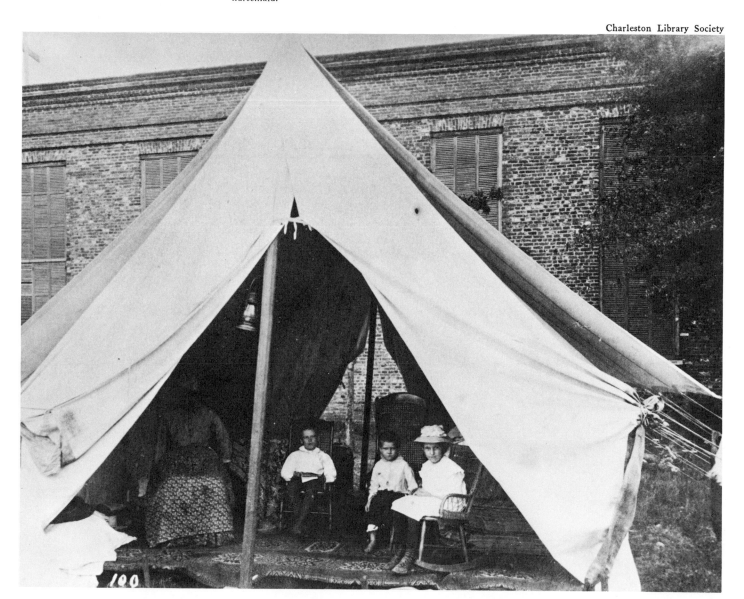

The Governor William Aiken house on Elizabeth Street was named after the man who made sizeable and grand alterations to the original structure after 1832. He added an art gallery in addition to installing interior ornamental work and building extensive dependencies. The Governor, the only son of the first president of the South Carolina Canal and Railroad Company, was a successful planter and served his state as chief executive from 1844 to 1846. Pictures on both pages date from 1893.

Governor Aiken's highly innovative real estate development on Wragg Mall is pictured below. He had seven identical dwellings constructed about 1845, and each one was expected to produce enough revenue to support his newly altered mansion one day a week. Known as Aiken's Row or more appropriately, the Seven Days of the Week, they stood in a line across from the Elizabeth Street entrance of the "big house."

Valentine Museum, Cook Collection

The elegant houses lining South Bay (South Battery) enjoy a pleasing view across White Point Garden. A horse-drawn car stands ready to begin its run up Meeting Street.

Trolleys were first introduced to Charleston in 1865, providing cheap and convenient mass transit for freight as well as for local citizens. The various lines were designated by the color of the cars. Even though two rival companies were in business they maintained the same system, using shades of slightly different hues; Broad Street was "the blue line." This was a particularly handy scheme, especially for those who could not read. Able to accommodate any traveler's whim, the trollies in the 1880's were busy nineteen hours each day, hauling passengers to within a short walking distance of any point in the city.

The fetching, crenelated structure pictured below in 1893 is the German Artillery Hall which stood on the south side of Wentworth Street between King and Meeting. Probably built from the proceeds of a lottery, it served as the military hall for the Fourth Brigade of the Second Division South Carolina Militia. However, its use was not limited to military purposes, and often the Musical Art Club presented several traveling artists in concert. The building was constructed in 1845 and "dismantled" in 1930. Its iron fence now encloses the front of the Gibbes Art Gallery.

West Point Mill Causeway in 1893 at the west end of Calhoun
Street depicts Charleston families relaxing on the promenade.
The goats pulling the children's wagons were treasured family pets.

In 1893 when this photograph was taken, the imposing residence was the home of Jacob Small. But historically, this dwelling at 18 Bull Street has come to be named after its first owner, William Blacklock. He was one of the successful merchant adventurers who came to Charleston from England after the Revolutionary War. And in 1800 he built this home in Harleston Village, an early suburb whose streets were initially laid out before the Revolution. The architecture of the Blacklock house marked an impressive debut of the style based on the designs of the Adam brothers of England.

This 1893 view of the Charleston Hotel on Meeting Street captures the beauty of its outstanding facade and colonnade of fourteen Corinthian columns. Charles F. Reichardt designed the hotel which had been the city's most fashionable stopping place since the early 1850's. The management went to great lengths to extend the greatest possible comfort to its guests. A June 1857 *Harper's New Monthly* article stated that the hotel's proprietor also directed Moultrie House, the summer refuge of Carolina on Sullivan's Island. And his "guests transfer themselves there and grow young in the embrace of the ocean, fanned with pleasant breezes from Ireland, Cuba, Cape Horn and other agreeable and equally near neighborhoods."

One year after this photograph was made a complete modernization program prompted the following remarks in a *New York Times* article entitled, "Six Hours in Charleston", which were reprinted in the *News and Courier* on March 15, 1892.

> The hotel with its old fashioned look, its big rooms . . . and new fashioned comforts that steam and electricity bring. . . . All these leave nothing to regret of the past, nothing to wish for the present . . . I do not believe that any newly built hotel could have rested me so much in so short a time.

One of the high points of Charleston's eclectic architectural epoch is reached right here on East Bay just above Broad Street. The Moorish facade of the Western Union Telegraph Company (formerly the Farmers & Exchange Bank) stands next to a classic Roman temple, the Planters and Mechanics bank.

Punctuating the skyline at regular intervals is the multi-tiered scaffolding of the utility poles. Undoubtedly the conveniences provided by these topheavy uprights compensated for their unsightly appearance.

The Chisolm Rice Mill at the west end of Tradd Street on the Ashley River was one of many mills constructed in Charleston as a natural adjunct to the Low Country's prosperous rice planting economy. Mr. Chisolm not only handled rice but he also milled lumber. His commercial colossus is pictured above in 1893.

Right—Little change is visible on Broad Street during the thirteen year period between these two photographs. The upper one was taken in 1893 and the lower one in 1906. The trees have grown some, and the trolley has been electrified. But four years hence in 1911 the building with the stately sidewalk colonnade would be replaced with a Charleston skyscraper, the People's Building, erected to bring business and prosperity to the city. Many local arguments arose about its height ruining Charleston's skyline, but these were somewhat abated when President Taft visited and announced that the view from the top of the building was worth it!

The date is Monday, June 28, 1897, and the members of the Palmetto Guard have assembled on Meeting Street to pose for the photographer before their annual parade to celebrate the British defeat at Fort Moultrie. They would march to the Battery and fire the customary salute at the Jasper monument, marking the 121st anniversary of this decisive Revolutionary War battle.

The young lady, dressed in white in the front row remembers the occasion in a different fashion. Two days earlier all Charleston trolleys were electrified, and that must have seemed a more reasonable purpose for a parade to a seven-year-old than a dreary battle of long ago. Her brother stands with her in the group of youngsters, and the two stylish ladies perched on the cannon, dressed in military uniforms, can be counted as kin. Major George Lamb Buist, a member of the Palmetto Guard, is also her grandfather so this can be best described as a classic example of "Charleston's closely knit society."

Anderson's Heavy Battery, marching to the ferry docks, was organized in response to a call for volunteers for the Spanish-American War. Edward Anderson of Charleston was elected captain after a corps of 144 had gathered from all parts of the state. Of the original 171 volunteers only 64 passed the physical; many were rejected on account of low weight including Captain Anderson! Historically Charleston men are sparely built individuals, though capable of great endurance, and a special telegram from the Governor to the President was needed to admit Captain Anderson.

The Battery was ordered to Sullivan's Island at the end of May where it remained until mustered out the following April 1899. The only change of station resulted from the heavy summer's rain flooding the parade grounds and threatening the health of the men; the entire Battery moved to the Isle of Palms until the situation reversed itself. Two fatalities occurred, one from typhoid fever and the other, the unsolved murder of a private on leave walking down King Street.

Franklin F. Sams Collection

The steeply gabled toll house on the Charleston side of the
Ashley River marshaled traffic over the New Bridge to Saint
Andrew's Parish. Always known by this simple monicker, the
bridge replaced the original one which had been burned in 1865
when Sherman's marauding troops were anticipated. However,
twenty-four years passed before the privately owned Charleston
Bridge Company spanned the river with the New Bridge. The
county purchased it in 1921, removed the toll, and five years
later constructed a modern, concrete bridge to take its place.

The family ox is a wonderful beast of burden. When he's not being used for farm operations he provides the family with wheels.

This quartet probably constitutes a Middleton Place tenant family employed in the phosphate mining industry. They are posed in front of the south wing, the only remaining portion of the stately Tudor style plantation house built before the Revolutionary War by the first Henry Middleton, who also designed its sumptuous formal gardens. A Yankee raiding party set fire to the house in 1865.

The phosphate industry was particularly profitable for Middleton and its neighbors, Magnolia and Drayton Hall, because the most workable land mines were located on the west bank of the Ashley River. The recovered minerals, used in the fertilizer industry, had rescued Charleston from a severe business recession.

The photograph can be dated after 1886 by the circular bolts which punctuate the brickwork between the first and second floor. These secured tie rods installed after the earthquake to stabilize damaged walls.

It was not until 1916 that the vast labors of returning the gardens to their original beauty were initiated.

In the early days of the century when automobiles were scarce, the faithful attendants at the annual service reached Saint James's Church at Goose Creek by a special excursion train arranged by the vestrymen. From the railway stop they rode carriages or buggies, or walked the sandy road to the church.

Serving the earliest Anglican congregation outside of Charleston, this colonial church marked the religious center of a once flourishing settlement of plantations. But times changed, and when this photograph was taken most of the good farm land had been depleted.

Statuesque live oaks draped with grey moss line Summerville's Sumter Avenue in 1906. Their serene appearance must have enhanced the community's reputation for rest and relaxation.

Summerville, twenty-five miles inland from Charleston, was originally populated by Low Country citizens who retreated there in the summer to escape the dreaded fever. Simple dwellings, suitable for just a few months' occupancy, made up the village, but by 1828 a more permanent population arrived. As Summerville grew, incorporation followed in 1847, but the town suffered along with the rest of the South after the Civil War.

By 1891 its reputation as a health resort grew nation-wide. Charleston's "suburb in the pines" was hailed by the Congress of Physicians, meeting in Paris, as one of the two best places in the world for sufferers from pulmonary diseases on account of "its pure, dry resinous air."

Pine Forest Inn, situated amid sixty acres of superb pines, provided outstanding accommodations for those attracted to Summerville by its promise of relief from pulmonary disease. Designed by S. A. Woods, a New York architect with vast experience in planning luxury hotels, Pine Forest Inn was a model of turn-of-the-century comfort. Captain F. W. Wagener of Charleston owned the hotel and all state visitors to the Low Country were entertained here. The photograph was taken in 1893.

The Hendersonville, North Carolina train station, pictured above in 1902, welcomed generations of Charlestonians on their annual summertime migrations, seeking relief from the Low Country heat and its accompanying swarms of disease-bearing mosquitoes. Enormous residential properties were developed in the North Carolina mountains and the South Carolina Piedmont during the nineteenth century, especially in the area round Flat Rock, which was known as the "Little Charleston of the Mountains."

The Chimney Rock excursion group has stopped to enjoy the spectacular view, and the thin mountain air must have induced a bit of giddiness . . . find the couple who have exchanged hats!

King Street is draped with buntings and banners to welcome
the Confederate veterans.

The handsome structure pictured left above, Thomson Auditorium, had
just been completed in time for the United Confederate Veterans' Reunion on
May 10, 1899. At that time a large portion of Charleston's economic base was
crumbling—the phosphate mines, the rice industry and Sea Island cotton. The
income produced by a large influx of people to the community was hoped to
prime the pump of prosperity. Instead of using John Thomson's recent bequest
to the city for straightening King Street, it helped to finance the new auditorium
building. The reunion was an immense success, attracting 30,000 people to the
community, who were entertained with a variety of activities, including a re-
enactment of the attack on Fort Sumter, which was staged on Colonial Lake.
The auditorium continued to serve as a meeting place for conventions until
it was taken over by the Charleston Museum in 1907. (See page 91.)

The interior of the auditorium contained seating accommodations for 8,000
people.

Montague Triest's photograph appears on his season pass book Number 197 for the South Carolina and West Indian Exposition, which opened on Sunday, December 1, 1901, and closed six months later on the last evening in May. The idea had been originally submitted to the *News and Courier* in a letter by Colonel John H. Averill, and it was hoped that the Exposition would bolster the Low Country's languishing economy. The solicitation for funds, construction of buildings and the management of the Exposition itself, represented a gargantuan effort on the part of Captain F. W. Wagener who headed the company which organized the project. It has been claimed that every Charleston citizen worked, even the children, towards the Exposition's success. Regardless of its long-range commercial value (and that may be questionable), the Exposition provided again another opportunity for Charlestonians to display their native optimism, devotion to their community and ability to work together.

Opening day was marked with the most imposing parade Charleston had ever witnessed. A message of congratulations arrived from the President of the United States. The band played "My Country 'Tis of Thee", the German Artillery fired a forty-six gun salute, and the Exposition opened! Pictured above, parade participants are forming on Marion Square.

Two Charleston sisters, Ruth and Lois, tour the Exposition. Here they are in front of the Administration Building, a glorious example of one of the grand architectural styles used throughout the fair. All roofs, domes, turrets and towers were tinted an ivory color, hence the colloquial name, "The Ivory City."

The girls' photographer, George W. Johnson, was also their father. He numbered among the local camera buffs whose hobby has afforded us a rare opportunity to "see" into the past life of a community. Mr. Johnson, according to a 1901 local commercial directory, was the grandson of the founder of a large umbrella factory on King Street. He had developed "superior connections with the manufacturers of the most popular makes of hats . . . and has the patronage of the best class of trade." So it would appear that George W. Johnson was successful in umbrellas and hats as well as in photography.

Right above—The United States Marines came to the Exposition, and the girls are visiting their camp.

Right below—Oregon sent a tree trunk whose enormous girth dwarfs Ruth and Lois. This exhibit in the Agricultural Hall hoped to establish commercial relations which would "hold a great future for this far distant Pacific state."

Their tour has come to an end in the Philadelphia Building. The girls pose on either side of the Liberty Bell. Little brother Sydney has arrived and he sits on top of it!

Left above—Ruth and Lois Johnson are strolling through the sunken gardens with its network of canals. The gardens occupied a small portion of the Washington Race Course grounds, and afterwards the city bought this section and incorporated it into the design for a new recreation area, Hampton Park.

Left below—The sisters admire the statuary which was especially designed to stand in front of the Negro Building. The sculptor, Charles A. Lopez, won a silver medal for his work and, by reputation, it was one of the finest pieces commissioned for the Exposition.

The children of the Charleston Orphan House and other spectators are all lined up on Calhoun Street awaiting the Liberty Day parade to pass by. The girls look especially sparkling in their well-starched pinafores.

The Orphan House dates back to 1794; the structure was greatly enlarged and remodeled in the beautiful Italian style we see above in 1855. Jones and Lee, a Charleston architectural firm, designed the renovations which included a modern steam heating system and space for a complete library. Generations of Charleston children found a home here, and many bestowed, in gratitude, the rewards of their later financial success to the city.

Left above—In an act of brotherly love, the city of Philadelphia constructed a building and sent down the Liberty Bell. Its arrival on January 9, 1902, accompanied by the Mayor of Philadelphia, was announced with a thirteen-gun salute. The photograph above was taken during the transfer of the bell from the railroad to the triumphal car which led the parade to the Exhibition grounds. The cart was drawn by thirteen horses and led by thirteen United States soldiers in full uniform.

Left below—A view of the grand parade honoring the arrival of the Liberty Bell

President Theodore Roosevelt chats with Charleston's Mayor Smyth aboard the Revenue Cutter *Algonquin* (photograph below) while visiting Charleston for the South Carolina and West Indian Exposition. After touring the Navy Yard, the cutter sailed down the Cooper River beyond Fort Sumter. The President's visit coincided with the anniversary of Lee's surrender on April 9. A parade was held in his honor, highlighted with the presentation of an Exposition Ode, music by Jules G. Huguelet and words by Sallie M. A. Black, entitled, "We Welcome President Roosevelt." Captain F. W. Wagener's dinner at Pine Forest Inn, Summerville, ended the President's stay in Charleston.

Carolina Art Association

Franklin F. Sams Collection

A group of exposition dignitaries are posed in front of the Woman's Building. This post-revolutionary mansion, Lowndes House, was owned by Captain F. W. Wagener, president of the South Carolina and West Indian Exposition. He donated his farm rent free, and the house was used by the Daughters of the American Revolution and the Colonial Dames to assist the weary and welcome women to "tarry a while sitte ye down, and have a cuppe of tea" (which was grown at the Pinehurst Tea Farm in nearby Summerville.)

The sign on the side of the Seed Store at 268 King Street just below Wentworth says that William McIntosh is the successor to John Thomson. This was the same Mr. Thomson whose generosity was responsible for the new auditorium named in his honor. (See page 74.)

Left—A group of visitors pause on the veranda of the New York Building.

Shortly after the Exposition closed at the end of May 1902, the "Ivory City" was dismantled and its airy castles disappeared forever. New industry did come to Charleston: the American Cigar Factory, the United Fruit Company, and an oyster canning establishment. And short-lived prosperity occurred. Between three and five million dollars were brought into the city; Charleston's hotels and boarding houses were filled to capacity, resulting in employment for hundreds of local people.

Charleston's oldest single house, c. 1720, is pictured in the left foreground of this 1906 view of Church Street just below Tradd. Number Seventy-one, Colonel Robert Brewton's house, exemplifies the floor plan indigenous to the city. The house is turned sideways on the lot, with its length running perpendicular to the front property line and its side, or gabled end, facing the street. The residence is one room deep, with two rooms to a floor; the entrance is located in the center of the house, midway along the piazza, which is approached from the street through a formal doorway.

The milk vendor pushes his cart carrying cans of various sizes to meet the needs of his regular customers. The universal bandana handkerchief hangs out of his back pocket, ready to wipe the lid of the milk can or a lump of mud from the wagon wheel.

Procedures for handling milk in the early century were rather casual in Charleston as they were elsewhere. Families kept cows in the city, disposing of any surplus milk to friends and neighbors; cleanliness was at a minimum and sterilization unknown. However, Charleston acquired another "first" in May 1919 when an ordinance was passed requiring pasteurization of milk, the first city in the United States to do so, preempting Chicago's claim to this honor by 16 years.

South Carolina Historical Society

Two "Ro Ro" (or "Roo Roo") boys, chimney-sweeps, armed with the tools of their trade, the brush and the scraper, stand smiling for the photographer. Working in pairs, the smaller boy would worm himself into the fireplace and up the chimney with the help of his companion. Once the job was completed, the young lad would announce this by sitting on top of the chimney and singing "Ro Ro" for all to hear. Their services were vital to the community because a dirty chimney was an extremely dangerous fire hazard.

90

The Charleston Museum's collection of artifacts from early Mediterranean civilizations, attractively arranged in the classical manner, occupied the top floor of the College of Charleston's main building. (See pages 35 and 53.)

The museum, the country's first, was founded in 1773, and its collections have been "on the run" ever since. Burned out of their original quarters at the Library Society, they were moved to Daniel Cannon's house on Queen Street. The collections were then housed for short periods at the Court House, a Chalmers Street building, and the Medical College before arriving at the College. Soon (1907) the Museum would take over the Thomson Memorial Auditorium, but unfortunately the stability of that building would later be questioned. Undoubtedly, the odyssey has not yet ended. (See page 74.)

Charleston Museum

Market Hall stands with majestic mien on Meeting Street, the protector of the three blocks of stalls stretching out to East Bay. This Roman temple, decorated with an appropriate frieze of bulls' heads, was not erected until 1841, many years after a public market had been operating here. The Pinckney family had given the site to the city shortly after the Revolution for a market, with the stipulation that the land would revert back to the family should it ever be used for another purpose.

Very much a part of the daily life of every Charleston family, the Market was governed by stringent ordinances issued by the city. These regulated not only the quality of its products but the hours of operation and the standards of sanitation; i.e., butchers' cuts and weights were inspected regularly, clean white aprons were the order of the day, and no produce could be brought to market for sale a second time. Market Hall is pictured below at the end of the nineteenth century.

The three-masted schooner *Warner Moore* pictured in 1907 was probably loaded with rice, which had been processed for shipment abroad at the West Point Mill seen in the background. Unfortunately, such commercial establishments would soon lose their importance in Charleston's economy, when the Low Country's rice fields were irreparably damaged during the severe storms of 1910 and 1911.

William Webb, Charleston-born in 1887, who served as a peripatetic deckhand during the first part of this century, remembers bringing the last load of rice to West Point Mill. This occurred about 1912 when he sailed with Captain Sam Guilds on the *Thomas Morgan*, and two lighters (barges), loaded with rice from Fairlawn on the Wando River, were towed to West Point.

The vista across Colonial Lake always evokes the same pleasurable response whatever the season or year. A 1912 view pictures a small fleet of rowboats moored to floating buoys.

Originally part of the Ashley River Embankment and Colonial Commons, an area deeded to the people of Charleston before the Revolutionary War, "The Pond" was dubbed Colonial Lake in 1881. Shortly after, concrete walls enclosing it and the terraced gardens forming the promenade were completed during the administration of Mayor William A. Courtenay.

Utilized by all of Charleston's citizens, Colonial Lake has earned its reputation as one of the city's most popular "pleasure resorts."

Number Four South Battery was built in 1893 by a dashing Charleston gentleman, Andrew Simonds, for his young New Orleans bride of a few years. This elaborate Italian Renaissance villa, built around an inner atrium which contained a marble pool, was luxuriously appointed in every respect. However, the family's fortunes changed, and the house became Charleston's famous Villa Margherita in 1910, six years after this photograph was made. It remained a fashionable inn for visitors to the city until after World War II when it was returned to its original use, a private dwelling.

Library of Congress, Detroit Photographing Company

King Street by night in 1912 is lighted with a series of dazzling arches which cross it at regular intervals as far as the eye can see. The Charleston Consolidated Railway and Lighting Company decorated the city's main thoroughfare in this fashion each year at holiday time.

Charleston had illuminated its streets over sixty years earlier on March 30, 1848, one of the first cities in the country to do so. The gas light had been introduced in Charleston by M. C. Mordecai and Joshua Lazarus (an ancestor of the M. H. Lazarus Company Hardware on the corner). Even after the Charleston Electric Light Company was formed in 1889, gas lights remained in use for some time on the city's smaller side streets.

The crushed oyster shell promenade along the Ashley River
in White Point Garden is lined with comfortable Battery benches
and shaded by the overhanging boughs of the live oak trees.
Commanding a splendid view of the harbor, this site has the
additional advantage of lying in the direct path of refreshing
ocean breezes. The city bought property here as early as 1830
for a public pleasure park, but the Civil War disrupted its final
development. At the time of this photograph, 1912, the earthwork
fortifications were part of the lore of "the late unpleasantness,"
and more than a few generations had already grown up romping
on White Point's Charleston grass and climbing the cannon.

Library of Congress, Detroit Publishing Company

The striking brick and wood gate denotes the entrance to a clapboard dwelling built in 1788 by one of America's first millionaires, Nathaniel Heyward. His older brother, Thomas, Jr., had already achieved colonial fame as one of the signers of the Declaration of Independence. Nathaniel's business success began with his marriage to Henrietta Manigault, a Charleston belle. This home served as the family's residence during the months spent away from their numerous rice plantations. The house was placed on land at the corner of Society Street and East Bay so that its occupants could enjoy a fine view across the marshes to the Cooper River.

Two families occupied the dwelling together quite comfortably during the 1870's and 1880's. But a succession of tenants and eventual deterioration subsequently spelled out its doom. The photograph below was taken before World War I.

A sight almost beyond belief—snow in Charleston—covers the city with a blanket of white! The young lady is fashioning a snowball in the yard of the Custom House on East Bay, identified by its distinctive iron fence standing in the background.

The Southern Fruit Company building across the way at 217 East Bay numbers among the host of Charleston's fine commercial structures that have disappeared. This particular one, a valuable example of Italianate architecture, was built c.1840 and torn down in 1964.

The roof garden atop the north wing of this Victorian mansion indicates a high degree of climatic innovation. A few Charlestonians still remember, with great nostalgia, the delightful summer evenings spent there catching the freshening breezes from both rivers and enjoying the serenity of its "heavenly" location.

Would you guess that within this dwelling at 60 Meeting Street lies a pre-revolutionary structure? The original house, c. 1740, contained two rooms on each of its three floors. The major Victorian facelifting was probably the work of its new owner in 1884, Bertram Cramer, a Charleston contractor. The double set of bays and the fourth story with its mansard roof were added sometime after this date.

A crowd has gathered on foot, on hoof and on wheels at Meeting and Hasell Streets to observe the fire department's efforts to douse the smoke spewing out of the St. Charles Hotel on the corner. From the time of the first settlement on the peninsula, fire has been a threat to the city and ever remains a constant enemy.

After 1740, the date of one of Charleston's destructive fires, and before the middle of the 1870's when the city fire department was organized, fire companies were formed on a "club" basis to protect Charleston's buildings. Membership was by invitation which carried with it the status of belonging to an exclusive social group. The men drew no salaries and bought their own uniforms. The alarm was rung on the bells of Saint Michael's and fire-watchers in the steeple pointed lanterns in the direction of the blaze.

The "vegetubble" lady balances her appealing, though weighty produce in a basket atop her head as easily as one dons a summer "straw." Winding her way along Charleston streets she announces her arrival in song, advising her regular customers to select from the carrots, beets and turnip greens seen poking out her basket. The produce varies with the season as do the accompanying lyrics, all rendered in a compelling chant:

Strawber-ry.......
    an e fresh and an e fine,
    an e just off the vine!
        or
Green Pease,
    sugar pea, red rose to-matoes!

Although Saint Michael's Alley in 1910 has a rather seedy appearance, a hint of its past can be discerned in the imposing building with the interesting gabled roof halfway up the lane. This is Number Eight, designed by Charleston architect, Edward B. White, and once the law office of James Louis Petigru, an outspoken opponent of secession whose famous epitaph is carved on his tombstone in Saint Michael's Churchyard around the corner.

Note the telephone pole at the corner topped with a can-shaped device which the neighborhood boys always chose for their favorite slingshot target.

South Carolina Historical Society

All Masons have a special interest in the building on the northeast corner of Broad and Church Streets occupied by Klinck, Wickenberg and Company's bustling wholesale grocery business. The first meeting of the Mother Supreme Council in America took place here in May 1801, and Solomon's Lodge No. 1, Free- and Accepted Masons, had also gathered on this corner some years before in 1736 (probably in a different structure.)

In the early days of Masonry, the craft was not confined to their secret good works but took a very active interest in public benevolence and in social and religious matters. Among their many civic services were included several financial contributions to the city after its numerous destructive fires.

In 1858 Charleston's art patrons organized the Carolina Art Association. Before it had a permanent home, rented quarters accommodated its sporadic efforts to make art instruction and appreciation available in the city. Despite the economic conditions after the Civil War, the association continued to grow.

Toward the end of the nineteenth century, a Chalmers Street structure known as the "Depository" was purchased. Its interior is pictured above showing Miss Fery (far right), the French instructress hired in 1894, with four of her pupils. The seated young lady is Alice R. Huger Smith, Charleston's renowned artist and author. Plaster casts stand in the background which were used for teaching models, and the association's acquisitions are hanging on the walls.

The completion of the James S. Gibbes Memorial Art Gallery on Meeting Street in 1905 marked an important milestone in the city's cultural history.

Fired with enthusiasm, the exhibition committee lined the walls of the new museum from top to bottom with almost the entire collections of the Carolina Art Association. Pictured below is the main gallery looking south, showing triple and quadruple tiers of paintings with the miniature collection in separate freestanding glass cases; statuary adorns the radiators. Classroom benches and an assortment of odd chairs reflect a meager budget.

Charleston's handsome Custom House stands in the background of this 1910 view from the Cooper River, looking toward the foot of Market Street. Tied up to the government docks are two lighthouse tenders, the *Wisteria* operated by Captain O'Brien and the *Mangrove* by Captain Touchstone. The Charleston headquarters for the Sixth District of the United States Lighthouse Service used these steel-hulled vessels to supply the lights up and down the coast with fuel and other necessities.

The wooden shed on the left protected the docks of the Mount Pleasant and Sullivan's Island ferries. The covering made it rather comfortable for the passengers, but the captain's skill was sorely challenged each time he had to dock the ferry within such close quarters.

Howard R. Jacobs Collection

Franklin F. Sams Collection

The third *Charleston* in 1906 lies at anchor in the harbor. She carried the first troops of the American Expeditionary Force to France during World War I and sailed the world over before being decommissioned in 1923.

Although the first *Charleston* completed an uneventful tour of duty, the second *Charleston* had a much more colorful, though short-lived history. Launched in 1888 she carried the remains of King Kalakaua of Hawaii to Honolulu after his death abroad. At the outbreak of the Spanish-American War she was directed to Guam Island in the Pacific to raise the American flag over that Spanish possession. After sailing into the harbor at Fort Santa Cruz and firing a challenge, the Spaniards sent out a boatload of emissaries who apologized for having no gun powder to answer what they deemed a friendly salute. Imagine their astonishment when the true nature of the visit was explained! After this bloodless naval victory, the *Charleston* sailed on to Manila Bay to join Admiral Dewey's fleet. There she became grounded on an uncharted reef and wrecked beyond salvage; her crew was forced to abandon ship.

Post-Courier, Charleston, South Carolina

The first modest offices of *The Evening Post* are pictured above in 1894 at 133 Meeting Street, the present site of the Gibbes Art Gallery. The paper was organized that year and purchased twelve months later by Arthur Manigault for $520. He brought in W. W. Ball as managing editor, whose strong editorial direction combined with good business management led the newspaper to immediate success.

A sure sign of success is the new quarters of *The Evening Post*, located a block farther downtown at 111 Meeting Street next to Hibernian Hall. A group of newsboys are shown standing outside the offices ready to deliver the latest edition. A year's subscription could be purchased in 1901 for $6.00! The newspaper's biggest competitor, the older *News and Courier*, was still at its 19 Broad Street address.

Post-Courier, Charleston, South Carolina

The "boys in the front room" who filled the editorial positions for *The Evening Post* are pictured in 1901. The grim and serious business of publishing a newspaper is apparent in their expressions. Thomas R. Waring, editor from 1896 to 1935, is seated on the left and Thomas P. Lesesne stands at the far right. A modern typewriter is evident on the table, but certainly the publishers could have provided a more attractive spittoon!

Post-Courier, Charleston, South Carolina

The "boys in the back room" who printed the newspaper are photographed in 1901 surrounded by type racks and other tools of their craft. The composing room of *The Evening Post* presents a rather clubby and intimate atmosphere, hindered not a whit by its vast, peeling ceiling.

The initials, U. S., on the gates of the Military Academy of South Carolina (the Citadel) indicate the occupation by federal troops of the buildings within the compound.

Citadel cadets guarded the city during the War between the States until 1864, when they went into active service and the Academy closed. After the evacuation of Charleston in 1865, Union troops moved into the Academy's buildings, and a large portion of the federal garrison was quartered there for over a decade. During this period the west wing burned; it was later rebuilt and used for faculty quarters after the Citadel was reopened.

A view inside the Citadel quadrangle, taken between 1865 and 1879, depicts Union troops ready for inspection, with a group of local spectators leaning against the columns in the background, making their own inspection.

Life in the barracks was spartan in style; a typical room is pictured. The mattresses which fit on folding metal-framed cots were stowed away each morning, and all the cadets' worldly possessions were contained in the cubbyholes above. Blankets were neatly folded on top of the cupboard with belts and bayonets hung from hooks on the side. The kepie (Civil War) hat worn by the cadets was given up by 1902.

Right—A cadet's life does have its lighter moments. A friendly game of cards provides some diversion, and Saturday afternoon free time is occupied with sampling the wares of the "newfangled ice cream peddler" outside the Citadel barracks on King Street, about 1911.

Library of Congress, Detroit Publishing Company

The most scenic route and, perhaps, the most comfortable means of traveling to Magnolia Gardens in 1907 was via the Ashley River. The *E. H. Jackson* with Captain Pregnall at the wheel brought visitors to the gardens during the spring months. A boat excursion along the lazy, meandering river, followed with a picnic lunch and an afternoon's tour through the gardens blazing with blooming azaleas, must have left a memorable impression on the visitor. (See page 4.)

The *Seminole,* one of the Clyde Line's Indians that plied the Atlantic from New York to Jacksonville was photographed by Robert Achurch. This progressive steamship company first established service to Charleston after the Civil War, using three surplus Civil War gunboats converted for freight and passenger use. The vessel, pictured below was one of four that was built in the 1880's, an all steel steamer outfitted with the most modern marine machinery. The *Cherokee, Seminole, Algonquin, Iroquois* and all the other Clyde tribes spelled magical adventure to those Charlestonians who were fortunate enough to travel upon their decks.

The "swift and elegant" sidewheeler *Sappho* is pictured about 1910 on one of her numerous three-quarter hour trips between Charleston and Sullivan's Island. A ferry trip was always an adventure, and this particular boat provided entertainment in addition. Designed with a sharp "V" bottom, she listed easily; a dozen water-filled barrels were maneuvered about her decks to achieve stability. This trimming-out process, which usually began when the *Sappho* backed out of the slip, was accompanied with impressive sound effects, and it never failed to fascinate the passengers.

As early as 1878 the *Sappho's* schedule was advertised in the City Directory with Captain Fitzgerald at the helm. She was finally retired in the early decades of this century and sank at her mooring on the Ashley River where she now lies, undoubtedly part of Charleston's vast land fill program.

The four-mile shuttle between Charleston and Sullivan's Island began in 1798 with a team of mules walking in a circle, providing the power to turn the ferry's paddle wheel. Sailing vessels were also employed; in 1828 the continuing succession of steam ferries began.

Franklin F. Sams Collection

Osceola's grave at Fort Moultrie on Sullivan's Island, marked by the ornamental iron fence, was photographed in 1900. The Seminole Tribe's war leader died here in 1838 during his imprisonment. He had been captured a year earlier in Florida while holding a conference under a flag of truce.

Shortly after his arrival, Osceola was invited to dinner by the captain of the ship that had brought him to Fort Moultrie. He was persuaded by his host's children to give a last war whoop, and all Charlestonians in the lower part of the city were terrorized by the horrifying sounds which issued forth that evening from the captain's house on Atlantic Street.

Dowling   On the Sands of Time.

If clothes make the man, then the bathing costumes of the day leave much to be desired, but let us hope, at least, that they were comfortable. The stalwart ten are posed on the sands of Sullivan's Island complete with boat, umbrella and man's best friend. The structure in the background may be the new Atlantic Beach Hotel in Atlanticville, which was constructed after the extension of the Seashore Railroad across the island.

The history of Sullivan's Island can be traced back to 1674, just four years after the first Charleston settlers arrived. Captain Florence O'Sullivan for whom the island is named and probably its first inhabitant, was charged with firing a cannon whenever a ship approached the river's mouth.

A legislative resolution passed in 1791 allowed South Carolina citizens who considered it "beneficial to health" to stay on the island for the summer. They were permitted to build cottages on assigned lots, paying rent of a penny a year. Thus began the annual summer migration from the mainland to the "oilun."

Attire for a lazy summer afternoon on the front porch of the island house reflects the general formality of social life in that era. Charleston photographer, William P. Dowling, took the photographs on both pages in 1896.

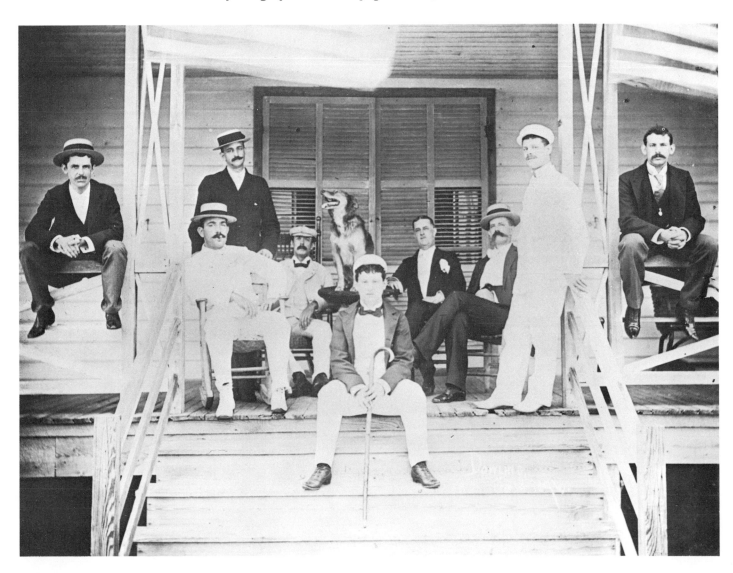

No better place to view the rooftops of Charleston can be found than from the steeple of Saint Michael's Church. In the background, signs of the city's economic development are evident in the smoking chimneys of Charleston's Neck, historically the industrial area at the northern boundary of the city.

The same view from Saint Michael's steeple is taken during one of Charleston's rare snowstorms.

The photographer, Robert Achurch, was another member of the Low Country's talented group of amateur "shutterbugs" during the early part of the present century. An Englishman and engraver by profession he came to the United States on the advice of his doctor. (Advice undoubtedly based on the stock-in-trade recommendation that taking a trip was the best prescription for improving one's health!) Mr. Achurch also sold Kodak cameras and supplies, carrying the sole distributorship in Charleston for many years.

Robert Achurch Collection, Charleston Museum

Post-Courier, Charleston, South Carolina

The August hurricane of 1911 "came in from the uncharted ocean" with winds of destructive violence at recorded velocities of 94 miles per hour. After the instruments at the Center Office of the Weather Bureau were damaged, higher readings were later recorded at the Charleston Museum (106 miles per hour at midnight on August 27). The tide rose five feet over its average level to 13.3 feet, and these two ferocious forces dealt their blows simultaneously.

Indications of the damage are pictured on these pages. Hardy souls have ventured out on High Battery to inspect the overturned Dahlgren cannon. On the opposite page, a view from High Battery looking north shows the churning waters of the Cooper River smashing against the sea wall.

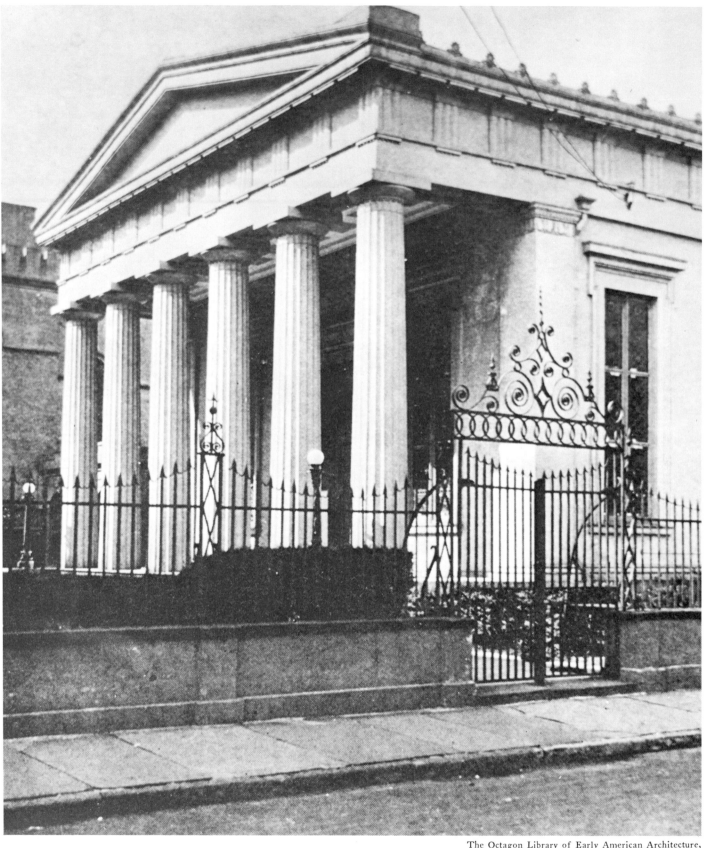

The Octagon Library of Early American Architecture,
Volume One Charleston, South Carolina—Albert Simons and Samuel Lapham, Jr.
c. 1970 University of South Carolina Press

Robert Achurch Collection, Charleston Museum

A cross section of King Street activity is viewed at the corner of Wentworth Street. The policeman converses on the sidewalk while the lady shoppers in their crisp white blouses, long skirts and plume-bedecked hats prepare to cross at the intersection.

The charming circular structure in the right foreground served as a freestanding display case for the retail business of Hirsch & Israel Company, located behind it. When the main building was razed some years later, the "gazebo" was moved to the residence of one of the owners on Rutledge Avenue and used as a summer house in the garden.

Left—The Synagogue of Kahal Kadosh Beth Elohim (Holy Congregation, House of God) on Hasell Street replaced earlier ones after the fire of 1838 leveled a large portion of Ansonborough. The Greek Revival style of architecture was at its height in Charleston; the new structure erected in 1841, from plans drawn by New York architect, Cyrus L. Warner, resulted in one of the most scholarly and well proportioned examples of that period in the city. Fortunately, the fine wrought iron fence was able to be salvaged and serves as one of the few remainders of the Georgian structure built by the congregation in 1794. Note the German Artillery Hall in the background. (See page 57.) The photograph dates from the early 1920's.

The Orangeburg banner, flying from the canopy post of the second automobile parked in front of the Timrod Hotel on Meeting Street, gives us a clue to the occasion. The annual Clemson-Citadel football game was held at the Orangeburg County Fair Grounds, and the convoy may be lined up to make a pilgrimage to that highly anticipated sporting event. The eighty mile drive took about four hours, so one hopes the group is enjoying a hearty breakfast in the hotel dining room before starting out. The vintage vehicles in the line-up include Model-T Fords and a few Buicks which date the photograph around 1910.

One of Charleston's more ambitious reclamation projects along the Ashley River is just about finished in this 1911 view.

The boulevard, contemplated by the city before the Civil War, did not get underway until 1909, when the forty-seven acres of mud flats from the west end of White Point Garden to Chisolm's Mill were filled in. At Andrew Buist Murray's suggestion the new boulevard was connected with the drive along East Battery, and he contributed a significant amount toward the cost of extending the sea walls to accomplish this. Mr. Murray, who grew up in the Charleston Orphan House, donated numerous gifts to the city, and the new boulevard was named for him, a fitting memorial to such a public-spirited citizen.

A small gallery of spectators is viewing a demonstration of the first official fire department automobile. The city council authorized the purchase of this twenty-four and one-half horsepower Buick in 1907 for the use of the fire chief; it predated Charleston's first motorized fire engine by two years.

The recurring ill health of the chief's horse had created such an annoying and costly problem that replacing the ailing animal with motor power certainly seemed a sensible solution.

Right—Favored family pets, the Charleston goats, are enjoying a tasty nibble on land behind the newly completed United States Post Office. Soon this "meadow" would be converted into a charming city park.

Across Meeting Street stands Saint Michael's Church with its splendid western portico. This outstanding ecclesiastical structure was finished fifteen years before the Revolutionary War. It has become not only a lasting symbol of colonial Charles Town and of the faith of the English settlers, but it has also served to display the superior ability of early local craftsmen.

Franklin F. Sams Collection

Streets and roof tops around the City Market are lined with buzzards. These "Charleston Eagles" were superior scavengers and thrived on the debris thrown in the streets by butchers from their meat stalls. Providing the city with its first solid waste disposal system, the birds were observed with great curiosity by citizens and visitors alike. In 1826, the Duke of Saxe-Weimar wrote:

> They are not only suffered as very useful animals but there is a fine of five dollars for the killing of one of these birds. A pair of these creatures were so tame that they crept about the meat market among the feet of the buyers.
> —George C. Rogers, Jr., *Charleston in the Age of the Pinckneys*

Over half a century later, Laura Witte Waring noted in her girlhood memoirs of Charleston from 1882-1895, *You Asked For It,* "A fine of ten dollars was levied for anybody running over a buzzard." The price has doubled!

The scene is the sidewalk in front of the Marine Hospital at 20 Franklin Street. Six Charleston damsels are "doin' the Charleston" in 1924 to the accompaniment of the Jenkins Orphanage Band. The building served as the children's home from 1895 until 1939 when the institution was moved to a farm on the Ashley River.

Robert Mills, Charleston's architect of prominence, completed the drawings for the hospital in 1831, and a series of these neo-Gothic structures were built across the country. He achieved a national reputation as architect for the Washington monument.

Post-Courier, Charleston, South Carolina

A pine-studded tract, six miles from the city on the old Meeting Street Road and resplendent with the healing virtues of country air, served as the site of Charleston County's first sanatorium. The red cross of the National Tuberculosis Association identifies "Pinehaven", the name chosen as most suitable from all contest entries submitted for a ten dollar prize. Under the supervision of "architect" Banov (Dr. Leon Banov, the energetic county health officer), volunteer builders and local workers, using World War I surplus material to stretch the county appropriation, completed the building in 1924.

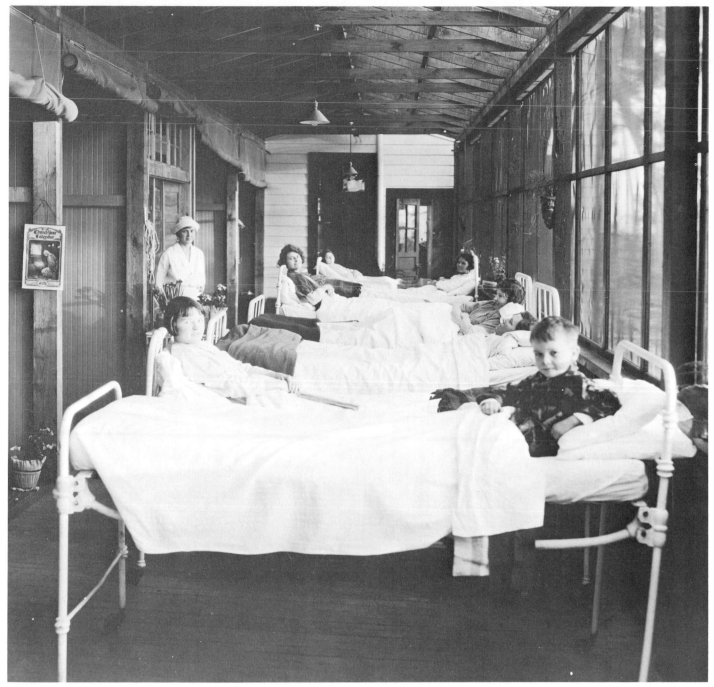

A view of one of the lateral wings of Pinehaven shows the open roof and screened-porch design which allowed the patient to spend a maximum amount of time out-of-doors at bed rest. Therapy for the disease before the discovery of antibiotics was essentially limited to this simple regimen. A quarter of a century later when this building was declared a firetrap, a new, modern facility was constructed in Charleston to replace it. After the move, one patient's remark may have echoed the feelings of the rest when he stated, "This ain't nothing but a hospital; we felt like it was home out there."

The haunting beauty of Cypress Gardens, located on Dean Hall Plantation, can be discerned from this photographic glimpse. The high ground has been planted with azaleas and other blooming flowers, creating an enchanting vista which is reflected in the dark mirror of the cypress swamps.

After the end of the rice economy, the fresh water preserves necessary for its culture reverted back to dense swamps. It was these wild woodlands that captivated Mr. Kittredge and his Charleston wife; they developed plans to domesticate the environment, resulting in this unique waterland garden which covers over 250 acres. Cypress Gardens was donated to the city in 1963.

The circus has come to town, and the elephant parade along
Meeting Street must have engendered enough enthusiasm to in-
sure a sellout for all Charleston performances. The automobiles
parked in front of the St. John Hotel (the Mills House) date
this photograph after 1927.

Two devastating tornadoes, fifteen minutes apart, swept across Charleston about eight o'clock on the morning of September 29, 1938, leaving twenty-eight dead and a two million dollar loss in property damage. The more severe of the two, of only three minutes duration, winged through the City Market almost from one end to the other. The photograph below looks eastward, along Market Street North. This was the first serious tornado since September 11, 1811.

Howard R. Jacobs Collection

The communicants who had attended the 7:30 a.m. service at Saint Michael's left just before the storm struck. The spire, main roof and trusses sustained injury, and other parts of the interior were badly damaged by the heavy downpour of rain that followed.

The City Hall, not seen on the photograph, but located to the far left (across the street from Saint Michael's) lost its roof also. All the window glass was broken but, fortunately, no serious damage was done to the Council Room's fine collection of paintings.

This view of the four masts of the *Anna R. Heidritter*, off East Battery, could be dated any time during the past century, but it was actually photographed on August 12, 1940, during the worst Charleston hurricane since the "Great Storm of 1911." The Captain displayed superior nautical skill by maneuvering the vessel to a safe anchorage in shallow water up the Ashley River. But unfortunately, she met her fate just a few years later in 1942 off the shore of Ocracoke Island near Cape Hatteras.

Right—The most insidious threat of all . . . the wrecker's ball swings free, ready to do battle with the colonnade of the Charleston Hotel in March, 1960. Perhaps a more judicious interpretation of "progress" would have saved it along with vast numbers of other noteworthy structures which met the same fate, leaving us needlessly impoverished. (See page 60.)

Post-Caurier, Charleston, South Carolina by William Jordan

Frances Benjamin Johnston, a master of the illustrated article in her time, would earn that same honor in today's world. She became one of the first news photographers in Washington at the turn of the century. After serving as the unofficial portraitist for a number of presidential administrations she began work in the field of architectural photography. In 1933, at the age of 69, when most of her contemporaries were content to be retired, she secured four consecutive Carnegie Foundation grants for a camera odyssey. This resulted in 7,648 negatives of buildings and houses in nine southern states. A selection of her Low Country photographs follows.

The entrances to Daniel Blake's tenements in Court House Square off Broad Street emphasize the colonial architectural innovation of raising the first floor well above street level, an adaptation to the local climate. Mr. Blake lived on one side and rented out the other, according to a January 10, 1771, notice in the *South Carolina Gazette*.

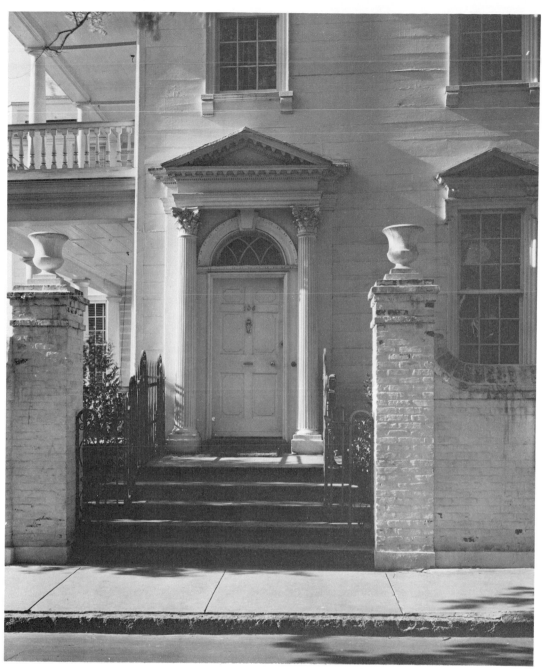

An outstanding Charleston doorway at 106 Tradd Street conveys the spirit of quiet sophistication which abounded during the city's pre-revolutionary golden age. Colonel John Stuart, the Indian Commissioner for the Southern Colonies, built this fine home c. 1772. The original drawing room woodwork was sold to the Minneapolis Museum of Art following World War I. At that time much of the wainscoting was restored. Exact replicas of the decorative friezes and carvings were installed in 1934 when John Mead Howells, the noted architect, renovated the house for his residence.

A conference which took place between Colonel Stuart and an Indian chief in the drawing room of this house was recreated in a three-dimensional diorama constructed by Robert N.S. Whitelaw, co-author of *Charleston—Come Hell or High Water*. This remains part of the permanent collections of the Charleston Museum.

Mulberry, so named for the bush which crowned the hill on which this "castle" was built, overlooks the Cooper River. Thomas Broughton constructed the dwelling in 1714, probably after the design of his family estate in England. Although Mulberry served as a neighborhood outpost during the Yemassee War, its four military towers followed the current architectural style, Jacobean baroque, rather than indicating the characteristic of a fortification.

Hampton on Wambaw Creek in the French Santee settlement dates back to 1735 when it began as a simple country house of six rooms, four on the first floor and two above. Two subsequent additions transformed it into a mansion of elegant proportions. The first included its famous ballroom and the last increased the front portico to the size shown in the photograph below. Completed in 1790-91, Washington's reception was held here when he stopped for breakfast en route to Charleston during his 1791 tour of the South.

Hampton was occupied by the Rutledge family from 1797 until the death in 1973 of South Carolina poet laureate and author, Archibald Rutledge. It is now owned by the state of South Carolina and will be maintained as an historic museum.